Reaffirm the Status Quo!

For Carolyn
Best from
Pat Oliphant

1997

Reaffirm the Status Quo!

More Cartoons by Pat Oliphant

Andrews and McMeel
A Universal Press Syndicate Company
Kansas City

_____ ATTENTION: SCHOOLS AND BUSINESSES _____

Andrews and McMeel books are available at quantity discounts with bulk purchase for educational, business, or sales promotional use. For information, write to: Special Sales Department, Andrews and McMeel, 4520 Main Street, Kansas City, Missouri 64111.

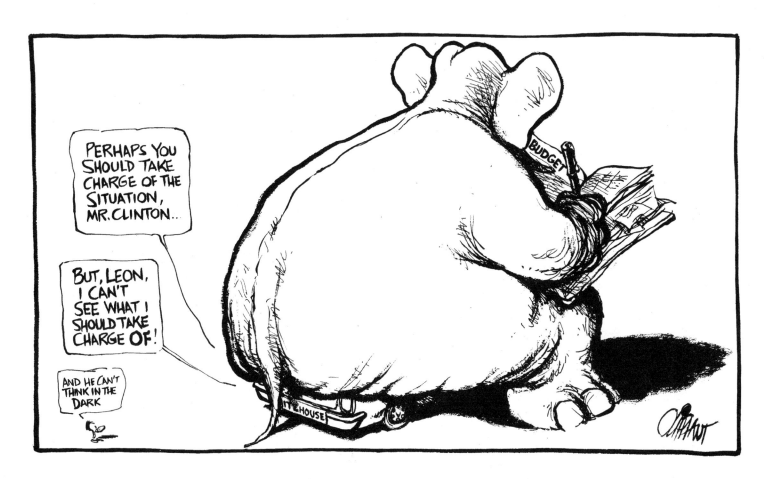

May 18, 1995

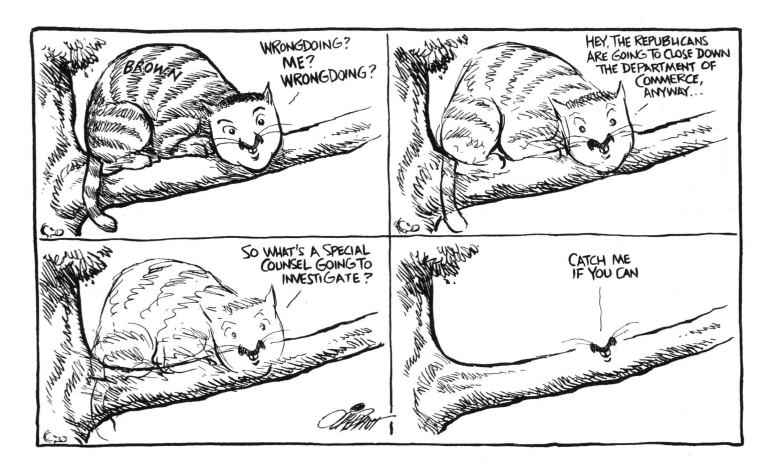

May 20, 1995

PENNSYLVANIA AVENUE, AND THE OPEN SOCIETY, ARE NOW CLOSED.

May 30, 1995

13

AND, NOW, FOR OUR NEXT HOSTAGE CRISIS...

'VIOLENCE IN ENTERTAINMENT—NOW, THERE'S A GREAT ISSUE!'

KING ROSS AUDITIONS THE CANDIDATES.

June 7, 1995

June 8, 1995

19

June 9, 1995

'THESE STUDIES ARE INCONCLUSIVE — SO FAR WE'VE ONLY SUCCEEDED IN GIVING CANCER AND HEART DISEASE TO LABORATORY HUMANS.'

June 12, 1995

21

June 14, 1995

SUPREME COURT JUSTICE THOMAS WRITES AN OPINION.

PATRIOTS.

June 21, 1995

June 27, 1995

29

June 28, 1995

THE POUNDING OF LITTLE FEET.

'...A LITTLE E. COLI, A SAMPLING OF SALMONELLA, ONE RANCID SIDE OF BEEF, MAGGOTY PORK, MORE FECAL MATTER, CARCINOGENS — WE'LL CALL IT "DOLE STEW".'

July 12, 1995

'AND IF THERE ARE ANY MIAs IN THERE, THIS IS PROBABLY THE BEST WAY TO FIND OUT.'

AT THE REPUBLICAN MUSEUM OF ART.

NEWT THE YOUNGER IS INSTRUCTED IN THE FINER POINTS OF STATESMANSHIP AND INTERNATIONAL DIPLOMACY BY HIS PERSONAL TUTOR AND MENTOR, DR. KISSINGER.

41

July 21, 1995

THE SEMI-INFLATABLE MR. JACKSON.

THE COMPUTERS ARE DOWN AGAIN AT CHICAGO AIR TRAFFIC CONTROL...

July 26, 1995

44

July 27, 1995

THE HAZARDS OF AGING.

45

August 9, 1995

'I'M IN A QUIRKY MOOD, JEEVES — LAY OUT MY RUNNING-FOR-GOP-NOMINATION SUIT.'

August 17, 1995

`MR. BRADLEY, WAIT! I'LL COME WITH YOU!'

AMERICAN JURISPRUDENCE (CONT.).

'I'M SHANNON FAULKNER'S REPLACEMENT, WHO TH'HELL ELSE!'

WINDOWS 95 — THE CHINESE VERSION.

August 24, 1995

'IT USED TO BE THE BANKERS WHO THREW THEMSELVES OUT OF WINDOWS, NOT THE EMPLOYEES...CHEERS.'

'JUDGE ITO WOULD LIKE YOU TO COME BACK INTO COURT, MR. SIMPSON — APPARENTLY THEY'RE STARTING TO GET SERIOUS AGAIN.'

'OK, BACK TO WORK! STOMP, STRIP, MAIM, MANGLE, TOPPLE, DISMANTLE AND DESTROY, LET'S GO!'

September 8, 1995

BOB SLOWLY GETS IT.

'YOU SHOULD BE ASHAMED! WHY, WHAT ON EARTH WOULD GENERAL POWELL THINK IF HE KNEW ABOUT THIS??'

September 14, 1995

AMERICAN JURISPRUDENCE: THE SIMPSON JURY, CIRCA 2,010 A.D..

OUT WITH THE BATHWATER.

September 20, 1995

69

WHERE'S COLIN?

SPEAKING OF TRAIN WRECKS...

THE HERO.

'NOW WE HAVE A MOTHER-DAUGHTER ENSEMBLE, FEATURING THE STARVING THIRD-WORLD SEAMSTRESS LOOK, SO VERY IMPORTANT IN TODAY'S FASHIONS...'

'FOLLOW ME!'

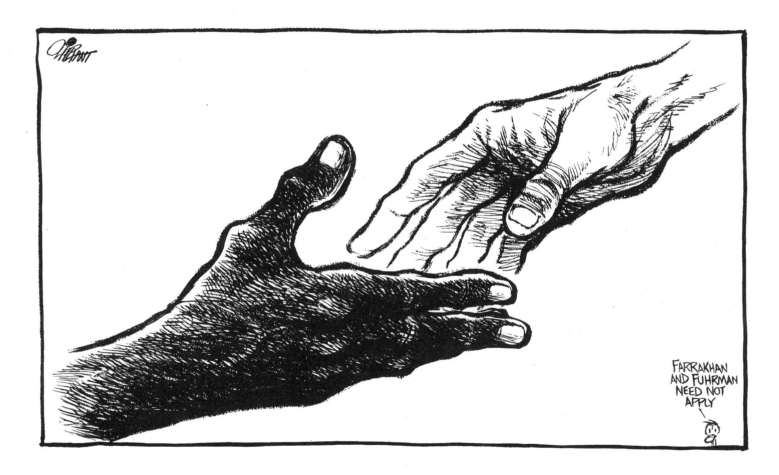

October 19, 1995

THE BIGGEST, MEANEST DOG ON THE BLOCK GETS HIS ORDERS...

'THAT'S NICE—THERE'S A CARD WITH IT, SAYS,'DEAR OCCUPANT.'.

'WELL, AT LEAST THEY'VE SHUT UP FOR A WHILE.'

November 3, 1995

83

November 3, 1995

'WASHINGTON SAYS GO AHEAD AND PLANT WHATEVER YOU WANT!'

November 9, 1995

89

THE GAME OF
CHICKENS AND
TURKEYS

TRAIN WRECK.

November 16, 1995

'AH, WILDERNESS, WHERE MAN HIMSELF IS BUT A VISITOR...'

GOVERNMENT 101.

November 23, 1995

95

"YOU THINK THIS IS BAD — YOU SHOULD SEE WHAT HE'S DONE TO HIS OWN HOUSE!"

'IT'S AGREED, THEN — FIRST, DEATH TO THE FOREIGN INVADER. THEN I'M GOING TO KILL YOU.'

December 2, 1995

PREPARING FOR HIS NEW, KINDER, GENTLER ROLE...

December 12, 1995

103

December 13, 1995

104

December 19, 1995

DEAR GOVT. FURLOUGHEE: THIS GOES TO THE ATTIC. THEN THERE'S THE BASEMENT TO CLEAN OUT.

107

HAZARDS OF SETTING YOUR OWN SPEED LIMITS.

December 27, 1995

111

THE PAYROLL FAIRY.

January 9, 1996

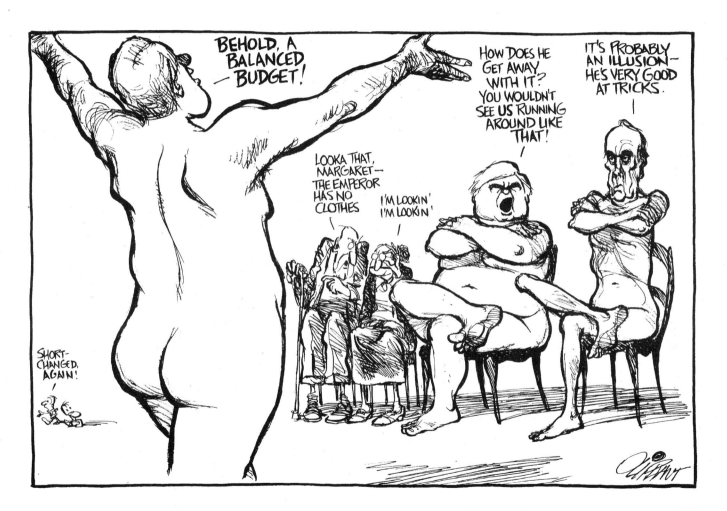

January 12, 1996

'TO HELL WITH PUBLIC OPINION — TELL CLINTON WE'RE GONNA SIT HERE UNTIL THE NEXT ELECTION!'

THE UPSIDE OF A FLAT TAX.

'WELL, WE'VE TAKEN OUR BALL AND GONE HOME... NOW WHAT DO WE DO?'

HILLARY'S KITCHEN.

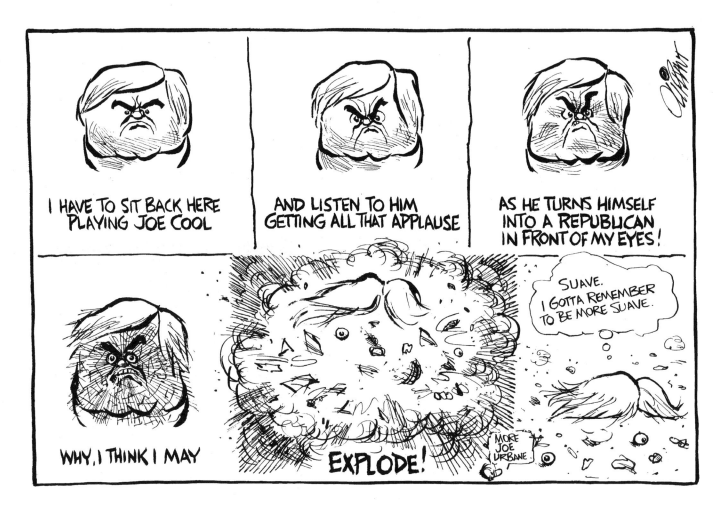

'WINDOW DOWN, THOMPSON... HI... STEVE FORBES...FLAT TAX .., RUNNING FOR PRESIDENT... VOTE FOR FORBES... WINDOW UP, THOMPSON.'

'BUT APART FROM THE CLIMATE, FOLKS, WHAT ELSE DO YOU LIKE ABOUT LIVING IN MINNESOTA..?'

'WILL THIS CREEP NEVER QUIT?'

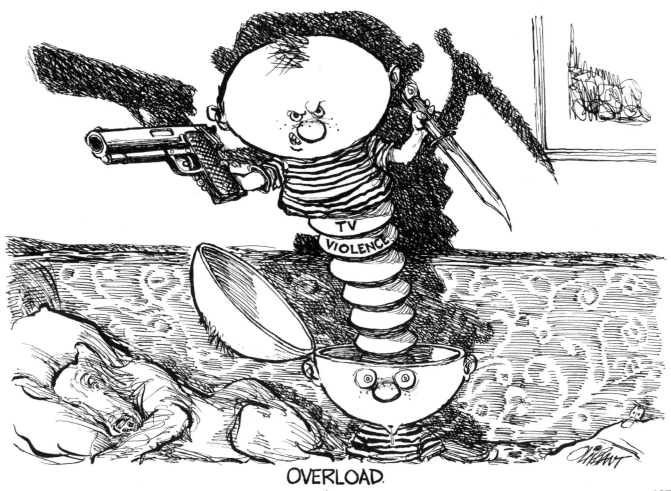

OVERLOAD.

February 20, 1996

THE CANDIDATE'S BAGGAGE

WHERE THE ELEPHANTS WENT TO DIE.

February 28, 1996

'HE SAYS HE'S GOING TO RUN FOR PRESIDENT ONE DAY, MAY THE GOOD LORD FORGIVE US.'

142

March 1, 1996

'ATTENTION! THE FOLLOWING PROGRAM ON PRINCESS DI'S DIVORCE CONTAINS PRURIENT MATERIAL UNSUITABLE FOR CHILDREN. YOUR TV WILL BE TURNED OFF. AND SIT UP. YOU HAVE TERRIBLE POSTURE. THAT IS ALL.'

'... MY DEEPEST SYMPATHY. YOURS TRULY, YASSIR ARAFAT.'

March 12, 1996

150

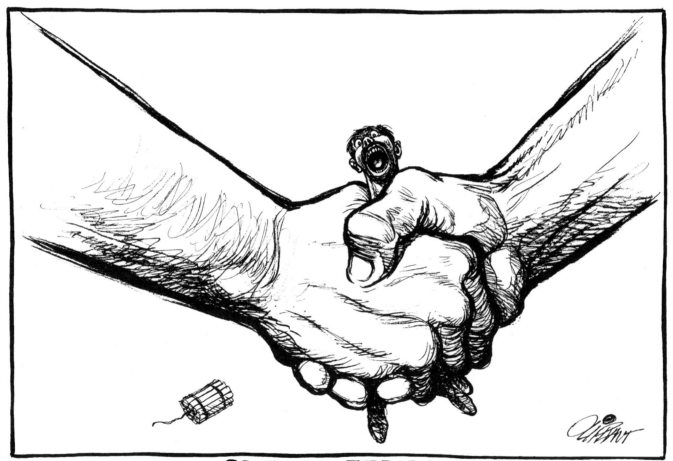

SQUEEZE ON TERRORISM.

March 20, 1996

156